W9-AEA-370

Baby Polar Bears

Bobbie Kalman

 Crabtree Publishing Company

www.crabtreebooks.com

It's fun to learn about Baby Animals

Created by Bobbie Kalman

For Bonnie Elizabeth Crabtree
We await you, our first granddaughter,
with much love.

**Author and
Editor-in-Chief**
Bobbie Kalman

Editor
Kathy Middleton

Proofreader
Crystal Sikkens

Photo research
Bobbie Kalman

Design
Bobbie Kalman
Katherine Berti
Samantha Crabtree
      (logo and front cover)

**Production coordinator
and prepress technician**
Katherine Berti

Illustrations
Barbara Bedell: pages 7, 18 (walrus and beluga whale)
Katherine Berti: pages 6 (map), 9, 24 (vertebrates)
Barb Hinterhoeller: pages 17, 24 (dens)
Trevor Morgan: page 18 (seal)
Bonna Rouse: pages 6 (polar bears), 14 (all except adult polar bear),
      24 (life cycle-all except top)
Margaret Amy Salter: pages 14 (adult polar bear), 24 (life cycle-top)

Photographs
BigStockPhoto: pages 7 (bottom), 13, 16 (top), 21 (top right),
      24 (mothers)
Dreamstime: front cover, pages 1, 3, 11, 12, 16 (bottom), 17 (bottom),
      22 (inset), 24 (sleeping bears)
iStockphoto: pages 7 (top), 21 (bottom)
Sue Flood/naturepl.com: page 20
Shutterstock: back cover, pages 4, 5, 6 (Earth), 8, 9, 10, 15, 18 (bird and
      polar bear cub), 19, 21 (top left), 22 (except inset), 23, 24 (all except
      mothers and sleeping bears)
Wikipedia: U.S. Fish and Wildlife Service: page 17 (top right)

Library and Archives Canada Cataloguing in Publication

Kalman, Bobbie, 1947-
      Baby polar bears / Bobbie Kalman.

(It's fun to learn about baby animals)
Includes index.
ISBN 978-0-7787-4894-6 (bound).--ISBN 978-0-7787-4899-1 (pbk.)

      1. Polar bear--Infancy--Juvenile literature.
I. Title. II. Series: It's fun to learn about baby animals.

QL737.C27K333 2010   j599.786'139   C2010-900824-3

Library of Congress Cataloging-in-Publication Data

Kalman, Bobbie.
  Baby polar bears / Bobbie Kalman.
      p. cm. -- (It's fun to learn about baby animals)
  Includes index.
  ISBN 978-0-7787-4899-1 (pbk. : alk. paper) -- ISBN 978-0-7787-4894-6
(reinforced library binding : alk. paper)
  1. Polar bear--Infancy--Juvenile literature. I. Title. II. Series.

  QL737.C27K3494 2011
  599.786'139--dc22

                                                            2010003035

Crabtree Publishing Company

www.crabtreebooks.com   1-800-387-7650

Printed in China/072010/AP20100226

**Published in Canada
Crabtree Publishing**
616 Welland Ave.
St. Catharines, Ontario
L2M 5V6

**Published in the United States
Crabtree Publishing**
PMB 59051
350 Fifth Avenue, 59th Floor
New York, New York 10118

**Published in the United Kingdom
Crabtree Publishing**
Maritime House
Basin Road North, Hove
BN41 1WR

**Published in Australia
Crabtree Publishing**
386 Mt. Alexander Rd.
Ascot Vale (Melbourne)
VIC 3032

What is in this book?

What is a polar bear?

Polar bears are animals called **mammals**. Mammals have hair or fur on their bodies. Polar bears are covered with white fur. Polar bears are **marine mammals**. Marine mammals live mainly in **oceans**. Oceans are huge areas of water.

Mammal mothers make milk inside their bodies. Mammal babies **nurse** from their mothers. To nurse is to drink mother's milk. These baby polar bears are nursing. Baby polar bears are called **cubs**.

Where do they live?

Polar bears live in the Arctic. It is their **habitat**. A habitat is the natural place where an animal lives. The Arctic is in the northern part of Earth, near the North Pole. It is made up of the Arctic Ocean and the lands around it. Some of these lands include Greenland, northern Canada, and Alaska. Find them on the map below.

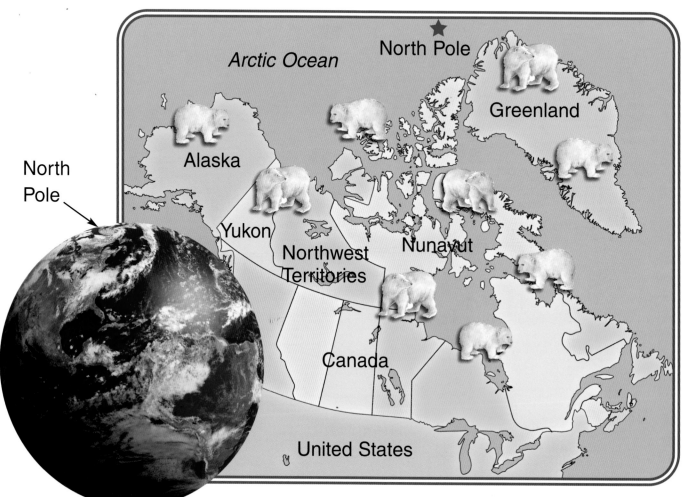

North Pole

Arctic Ocean

North Pole

Greenland

Alaska

Yukon

Northwest Territories

Nunavut

Canada

United States

Most polar bears live on **pack ice**, or thick pieces of ice that float in the ocean. In summer, they move onto land to find food. Their land habitat is called the **tundra**.

These polar bears are on pack ice.

The tundra is a cold, dry place where no trees grow. In summer, flowers and other small plants grow on the tundra.

Polar bear bodies

Polar bears are the biggest bears. Like all bears, they can walk on all four legs. They can also walk on just their two back legs. Polar bears have five toes with **claws** on each foot. Claws are curved nails.

Polar bears can smell, hear, and see very well.

White fur covers their bodies.

claws

Polar bears are **vertebrates**. Vertebrates are animals with **backbones**. A backbone is a row of bones down the middle of an animal's back. All the bones in an animal's body make up the **skeleton**.

This drawing shows a polar bear skeleton. The bones of the skeleton hold an animal's body together.

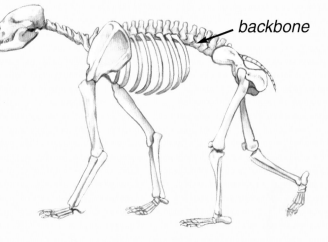

backbone

pad

A polar bear has large **paws**, or feet. The bottom of its feet have pads. The polar bear's claws and pads keep the bear from slipping on ice and snow.

polar bear footprint in snow

A polar bear's coat

Polar bears have two kinds of fur. Some of their fur is short, and some is long. Their short fur is next to their skin. It keeps them warm. Their long fur keeps water away from their skin. The fur of polar bears is thick and white, but their skin is black. You can see this cub's black skin around its nose, mouth, and chin.

Thick fur keeps polar bears warm and dry, even in the coldest weather. A cold wind is blowing, but this bear cub does not feel it, even though she is standing up.

Polar bear families

A polar bear family is made up of a mother bear and her cubs. Most polar bear mothers have one or two cubs that are born at the same time. This mother polar bear has two cubs.

This mother bear has just one cub. What do you think the cub is saying to her?

Mother bears protect their cubs from danger. This mother sees a male polar bear, which might try to eat the cubs. She is hiding the cubs with her body.

13

Polar bear life cycle

Each polar bear goes through a set of changes called a **life cycle**. A life cycle starts when a cub is born. The cub grows and changes until it becomes an **adult**. An adult polar bear is fully grown and can make babies. These pictures show the life cycle of a polar bear.

Adult polar bears can make babies.

A newborn polar bear cub cannot see or hear.

The two-year-old cub learns to feed itself.

The three-month-old polar bear cub learns to hunt and swim.

Growing and changing

A mother polar bear feeds her cub and protects it. When the cub is about three months old, the mother bear teaches it to hunt and swim. The cub still nurses until it is about two-and-a-half years old. By then, it knows how to feed itself.

Leaving Mom

The cub leaves its mother when it is about three years old. It is not yet an adult. Female polar bears become adults when they are five years old. Male polar bears become adults when they are about six years old. Adult polar bears live alone, except adult females with cubs.

Polar bear cubs play fight and chase each other. Playing this way teaches them how to defend themselves.

Sleepy bears

Adult polar bears spend most of their time resting or sleeping. They rest because they need to have energy to walk, run, hunt, and swim. A polar bear may swim as far as 62 miles (100 km) to find food.

These cubs are having a rest with their mother.
The one on the right is getting some sun on its belly while it sleeps.

Polar bear cubs are born in winter. Before the cubs are born, the mother bear digs a home called a **den**. The den is warm and safe. After the cubs are born, the mother mostly sleeps. The cubs nurse while their mother sleeps.

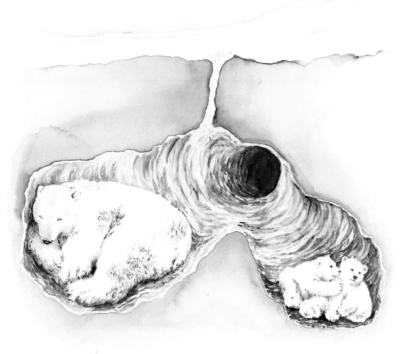

These baby polar bears are inside their den.

This mother bear is resting while her cubs are nursing. The family is outside the den.

Polar carnivores

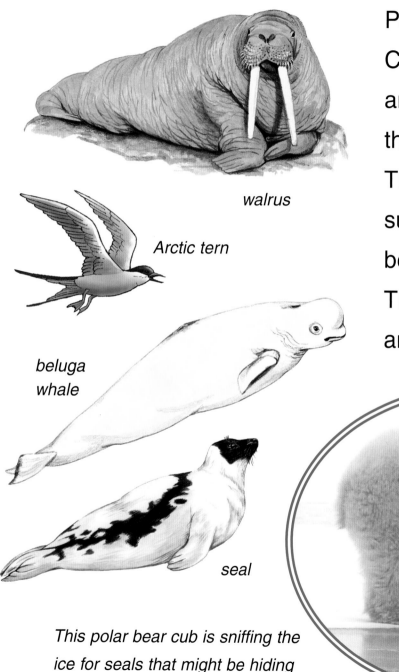

walrus

Arctic tern

beluga whale

seal

Polar bears are **carnivores**. Carnivores eat mainly other animals. Polar bears spend the winter hunting for food. They hunt and eat animals such as walruses, narwhals, beluga whales, and seals. They also eat sea birds and bird eggs.

This polar bear cub is sniffing the ice for seals that might be hiding underneath. She is very hungry.

These polar bear cubs have found a dead whale to eat. It will feed them for many days.

*These bear cubs could not find any animals to hunt, so they are eating **kelp**. Kelp is seaweed that grows in oceans. Polar bears usually eat meat, but these cubs are hungry.*

What is a predator?

Polar bears are carnivores. They are also **predators**. Predators hunt the animals they eat. Polar bears are the top predators in the Arctic. Top predators eat smaller predators, such as seals. Without top predators, too many smaller predators would eat most of the other animals. Soon, there would not be enough food for all the Arctic animals to eat.

This young polar bear has spotted a beluga whale too late. It got away!

These seals have come out of the water to sun themselves on an ice **floe**, or piece of ice.
A polar bear is hiding in the water near them. Will he catch a seal for lunch?

This polar bear mother and cub have just eaten a seal.
The mother is licking the cub's face clean.

Danger ahead!

Polar bears need to hunt on ice, but the Arctic is becoming warmer. The pack ice is thinner and is melting earlier in the year than usual. Melting ice forces bears to come onto land, where they cannot find enough food. Some polar bears are starving.

The polar bear cub on the right is jumping from one ice floe to another. The ice floes are very small and thin.

The polar bear on the left is stuck on some floating ice and will have to swim far to reach land. Polar bears can get tired and drown during very long swims.

These polar bears are looking for food in a garbage dump in Manitoba, Canada. Bears search for food close to cities when they cannot find enough animals to hunt.

Do some research on the Internet and find the zoo nearest you that has polar bears. Ask your parents if you can visit and watch these beautiful animals in action. Then write your own story or poem about polar bears and read it to others to let them know how amazing these animals are. You can help polar bears by telling others about them.

Words to Know and Index

bodies
pages 4, 5, 8–9, 13

dangers
pages 13, 22–23

dens
page 17

food
pages 7, 16, 18–19,
20, 22, 23

fur
pages 4, 8, 10–11

life cycle
pages 14–15

mothers
pages 5,
12–13, 15,
16, 17, 21

nursing
pages
5, 15,
17

Other index words
Arctic pages 6, 20, 22
carnivores pages 18, 2
habitats pages 6, 7
hunting pages 14, 15,
   16, 18, 19, 20, 22, 23
ice pages 7, 9, 21, 22
mammals pages 4, 5
predators pages 20–21

sleeping
pages 16–17

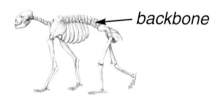

backbone

vertebrates
page 9